Spirit Within

Spirit Within

And Other Poems

Doris Ervin

All worldwide rights reserved. No part of this work may be reproduced without written permission of the author.

Spirit Within and Other Poems

ISBN-978-0-692-80569-5

This book is copyright material and cannot be copied, reproduced, transferred, distributed, leased, licensed or publicly performed or used in any way except as specifically permitted in writing by the author, as allowed under the terms and conditions under which it was agreed or as strictly permitted by applicable copyright law. Any unauthorized distribution or use of this text may be a direct infringement of the author's rights and those responsible may be liable in law accordingly.

Published by Doris Ervin
Denver, Colorado
USA

© 2016 by Doris Ervin

For All Who Seek and Wonder

CONTENTS

Acknowledgements ix

Sprit Discovering Self

Rebirth	1
Self-Realized	2
Dance Awakened	3
Pain Burning	4
Transformation	6

Spirit in the World

The Hunter	9
Energy Is	10
Interview	11
Spirit Within	12
Death of a Star	14
From Where I Stand	15
Us Together	16

Spirit in Nature

Wind	19
Side by Side	20
Sacred Places	22
Sunrise	25
Aspen Green	26
Reverence	28
Rocks from the Desert	29
Chihuahuan Desert	30

CONTENTS

Spirit Returning

Now I Lead	35
Weeds and Roots	36
Millie	38
And the Grass Turned Green	40
Too Whom Much is Given	44
I Knew	46
He Killed Her	48

Epilogue

I Am	53
Reflections	54

Acknowledgements

When I think about my poems, I link each of them to a moment in time. A moment like no other: a moment of shock, profound realization, great loss, great joy or great beauty. A moment that propelled me into action: to write a poem.

A similar moment that inspired me into action, occurred when the author, Joanne Brand, came to my community book club to talk about her latest book, *Dancing To Memories*. Brand is a dynamo of 'can do' attitude transformed into action. Joanne's 'can do' attitude, along with a commitment to her art, inspired me into action. Thank You, Joanne for being the inspiration to, 'just do it'!

Once the decision to 'just do it' is arrived at with full conviction, then, the nuts and bolts, in this case, technical steps, begin. Enter please, Barbara Duckworth. Barbara jumped in and helped to figured out the technological format required by the publishing platform. Thank You, Barbara, for your patience and encouragement.

A Thank You to my friends and family who have supported my poetry over the years. A Thank You, in memoriam, to Erla L. Lutz who will always be an inspiration and a moment in time.

Doris Ervin
Denver, Colorado
November, 2016

Spirit Within

Spirit

Discovering

Self

Rebirth

Rolling in mud,
body encased in
shell of earth and water.

Sun-fired, molded
matter enclosing
flesh and soul: Water
evaporates into air.

Mud-sculpted shell cracks
revealing new life.
Flesh and soul reborn
again, from the womb of
centuries-old matter, so dense
as to create a visual form.

Flesh and soul from flesh, or
flesh and soul from
earth, air, fire and water?

Self-Realized

Suddenly,
an ember ignites in
self-combustion. Breaking
into a steady flame, red,
orange, yellow and blue.
Rising skyward, defying gravity,
a combination of elements,
manifesting and experiencing
the uniqueness of form.

Smoke lifted upward
from a flaming cinder,
continuing the essence of fire.
White smoke, swirling, circling,
fading into infinity.

Two strong strands of smoke
emerged. First, one moved
toward the other, then,
in response, a momentary
merging. Just as quickly,
apart again, stronger from
the union, each seeking
its own expression.

Rising steadily together,
repeating the dance
farther from the warmth of
the fire but stronger still.

Dance Awakened

Ancient rhythms pulsating
in full bodied vibration
sounding a remembrance.

Ear perceiving
sound turning fluid,
flowing freely through
the body enslaved.
Feet alive with
unconscious movement.

Thousands of feet pressing
time over centuries;
ageless, wordless wisdom
carried on the souls of us all.

Pain Burning

Cylinder of heavy black, enclosed,
aflame with a single, spiraling ember
searing through black molecules.

Left in the wake of flaming,
searing pain, unknown form
in random order, without pattern.

Steaming ember
reaches the top of the cylinder
covered with layers of 'Heart' skin.
Ember sticks and begins to burn
from the inside, layer by layer.

Strength of ember,
burning with red, hot flame.
Delicate 'Heart' skin is
pink with innocence.
Heart freezes at first contact
with burning pain.

Soon, drops of water begin to fall,
through newly arranged molecules,
to the bottom of the cylinder.

A rushing waterfall
fills the cylinder,
deep, liquid pool,
interspersed with heavy black.
Falling water creates sound and
motion, where there was none.

Burning pain
rising through frozen heart,
releasing into White Light.

Heart, thawed,
once again returning
as the Mother of all life.
Molecules dispersed,
rearranged, realigned,
again creating spirit
in the physical form of life.

Transformation

Crawling in from the desert,
belly blistered from
scorching, dry, cracking sand.

Abandoned by Father Sun,
piercing rays into gaping wounds.
Mother Earth, too, withholding
gentle, loving acceptance.

Fruitless, waterless ego
parched beyond recognition.
Perspiration long since dried
into brown, powdery dust.

Blessedly, day turns into night,
the long arm of Spirit extending
into the deepest recesses of the soul.

Flicker of White Light in
still desert darkness,
a faint recognition,
remembrance.

Desert spring trickling
memories of Home.
Spirit bridging separated ego
Home to Soul.

Earth weary ego,
longing to relinquish control,
rolls in desert spring water,
purifying and releasing into Spirit.

Spirit

in the

World

The Hunter

Armed with nothing –
bare of foot, walking
gently upon the Earth:
a hunter of spirits,
lives past and future.

Listening
for the faintest crackling or
rustling of remembrance.

Seeing
any hint of the familiar:
color, movement, shape.
The eyes perceive in
concrete what the senses
translate into spirit language,
beyond language.

Flesh, the predator,
stalks experience
in transgression
to perceive more,
always in search of
the "Big One," the
trigger that fires the shot:
a dream that brings in
the trophy, rings in the ears
of all lives calling them
to the feast, the Present.

Energy Is

Continuous energy swirls,
one moment forming a tree,
a bird in the sky, or me.

That's why
I feel pain when the tree is
sheared off at its base, or when
bird falls from the sky,
wasted by a sportsman's bullet.

As part of the wholeness,
how can I ever be complete as
long as the trees and birds fall?

Without them I cannot be whole.
The part of me, my energy, that
extends to another, becomes
disharmonious, incomplete.

Without the tree,
I can never be as
strong and grounded.
Without the bird,
I can never be as free.

The Interview

Ancient money handler,
keeper of the purse,
now a modern banker.

Minority to minority.
Young African American man,
middle-aged Caucasian woman.
Working hard to prove ourselves
in roles non-traditional.
How far will we go?

"Do you have a killer instinct?"
he asked.

"I hope not,"
I replied.

Murderer, I thought.
Killer of compassion,
honesty, trust, integrity.

"No passion," he reacted.
Adrenaline arrested,
swordless service.

"We get the money first,"
he said.
Celebrate in the spoils!
Then, carry off the body.

Spirit Within

In the beginning
I drew a line that was me.
Gradually, from that line
there came more. In a
web of lines none being
predominant, I lost my way,
the original line that was me.

In confusion, I followed
first one, then the other,
each turning into another.
With a sense of urgency,
I tried to travel them all.

Finally, lost, exhausted,
I began to slow through
the curves and turns,
coming to rest
somewhere in the maze.

Lying on the earth,
belly down, arms outstretched
I shared my burden of
exhaustion and confusion.
The Sun, barely a shimmer
through the cover of clouds,
slowly warmed me.

The Earth,
in all her nurturing strength,
supported me through healing.
With a gentle nudge
She awakened me to the
Sun rising in the east.

As my head lifted
toward the light and warmth,
I knew I had been found.
When I looked around,
there was only one line and
it was me.

Gone was the maze,
I caught a moment in the
'No Time' at the end of the
stroke of the eternal pendulum.

Finding my strength,
I stood to full height extending,
both, to the center of the Earth and
into the infinite galaxy.

Stretching my legs,
I moved with ease
striding forth, lighter.
One with the strength of
Mother Earth, and the
light and warmth of
Father Sun, I encountered
no resistance.

Having remembered the line
that is me, I draw my own map.
I travel at my own speed.
Inspired by trust and belief,
I move with courage.

Death of a Star

A young boy took a photograph of an
unexplained astrological phenomenon:
a ball of fire streaking across the sky.

After much local speculation, NASA
agreed to study the photograph. At last,
an announcement: the boy, quite by
accident, had captured the death of
a star on film. Science, once again,
proclaimed a truth to us.

But, alas!

Scientists do not know
that stars don't die. They are forever.

Scientists do not know
that stars unceasingly beam clear
White Light to this troubled Earth.

Scientists do not know
that stars may reconfigure, recompose
or reposition themselves in the universe.
But, they never, ever, die. They just are,
beyond linear limits of life, death and time.

Scientists do not know
that this particular star is the young
boy's guiding light, making an
unforgettable introduction to him.

From Where I Stand

When I stand
at the edge of the ocean
where water meets land
I am drawn into the
sea of the great unknown.

Carried away by the infinite
power of motion, my eyes rove
the horizon, searching for
land-locked stability.

Deposited on the valley floor,
as if a bird had dropped a seed,
my spirit soars to the highest peak.

Anxious to meet
my clearest breath,
that place closest
to the clouds where
jagged, snow-covered, peaks
meet billowy, soft clouds.

Again,
I long for the security
of the valley floor.
"The desert," I say,
"Give me the smell of sage and
vistas of subtle colors."

"Do I favor the expansiveness of a
solid more than the lightness of air?"

Us Together

Somewhere, I read:
we cannot leave
this Earth in an elevated
state of consciousness
alone.

Our brothers and sisters
must be with us,
like a mosaic we
complete together.

I cannot leave
without You and
go anywhere.

An aspect of me
craves You; is
inseparable from You.

In the mosaic,
our sides bleed
into each other,
completing the whole.

I cannot run ahead,
I must wait for You.
I cannot lag behind,
You must wait for me.

Spirit

in

Nature

Wind

Invisible energy stirring
without or within?
Sensing movement,
gentle cooling breeze or
violent, twisting gale?

Unseen cause bending
grasses and trees.
Pushed or pulled?
Innate response to
an ageless call.

From whence thou come?

From the east?
Rays of sunrise blowing
inevitably towards twilight.
Days ebbing in
cyclic certainty.

From the north?
Cold winter winds blending
into warm, summer currents.
Seasons following the sun:
swirling, lifting, sifting out,
changing, renewing, purifying.

Side by Side

Deep
in the Rocky Mountains.
My eyes followed the
highest ridgeline, as if
reading a line in a book,
from left to right.

Soon, I saw more
than my eyes could
comprehend: lean, jagged,
skyward-thrusting peaks
free-falling downward
dramatically like
a child's erratic,
up and down scribbles.

In the absence of a distinct,
substantial valley floor, the
tireless form repeated
again and again:
a marathon of activity over
the eons.

Suddenly,
the dramatic, eruptive
cycle broke. Relief.
The ridgeline settled
into a peaceful, serene,
harmonious gradient.
A mountain replete:
outwardly rounded, inward
fissures filled, lone spiraled-peaks
worn down and lovingly absorbed
into the heart of the mountain.

The jagged,
unpredictable,
edge of youth turned
into wisdom of life,
worn and mellowed, all
reflected in a single visual:
one transcending
mountain range.

Two extreme aspects,
side by side, for me to see;
displayed against a vivid
blue sky as backdrop
for an infinite,
purposeful timeline.

Sacred Places

How they stand there
on the north slope of the
mountain, as if in stadium
seating, the top of one peering
out over the top of the one below.

As witness
to an ever changing world,
each with the best seat in the
house, a clear view of life being,
day by day, year by year.

Straight, strong and tall
through it all. The natural events:
wind, rain, drought, blizzard, fire--
Each, as if by divine design, to leave
them leaner and stronger still.

But, there are other events
man-made events:
he cuts them down, like
declaring war upon a pacifist nation.
He hauls the spoils away.

He profits.

Clearing complete, he pours
cement cold parking lots for
his most prized possession, and
his disposable litter is ever present.

An appetite without restraint.

He even kills
those creatures who roam freely
amongst them to hang in the
family den as trophies.

His ego soars.

He uses them as fuel for atmosphere
in hilltop mountain homes,
reducing them to smoke and ashes
for another's momentary pleasure.

Hilltop mountain homes –
trees turned into sticks, turned
into houses, now dot the ridgeline.
Evergreen silhouetted horizon gone
as the coveted last row in the
natural seating arrangement.

Gone are those who quietly rose
through the ranks to participate
in world events: their vision
unobstructed, their wisdom sure,
their energy clear and pure.

What happens now?
When Man occupies sacred places,
trees holding consciousness of
White Light for the world,
exchanged for man holding
consciousness of materialism?

Man conquers nature once again.
We live the consequences:
day by day, year by year,
in war after war amongst
ourselves, world over, in our
spiritless, material existence.

Sunrise

I drove west,
out of the city into
the mountains, on a
sleepy Sunday morning.

Then, a glimpse of sunrise
colors in my rearview mirror:
orange with undertones of
flaming red, travelling across
the universe in response
to an ancient, timeless call.

Simultaneously, a local radio
station announcing a gorgeous
sunrise like breaking news.
My inclination: to stop and partake of
the majesty of a waking universe.

On the Interstate,
forced to drive straight ahead,
I could only observe a mirrored
reflection of a live event.

Mechanically propelled forward,
but soulfully pulled backward.
Should I pretend something
magnificent was not unfolding in
the eastern sky behind me; remain
blind to indescribable beauty?

It was painful, the inability
to witness, to engage in, to give
complete, undivided attention to
such a miraculous event.

Aspen Green

Brilliant,
crisp, yellow
deepened into gold by red.

White-trunked,
clustered communities
shimmering celestial hues
against a sky of clear blue.

There
amongst the gold and red,
stand those still green,
yet to burst into their
own autumn splendor,
unlike most, so eager to
transition into the new season.
A few, even, jumping out fast past
gold to red impatient to display
themselves in raucous, wild delight.
An annual rite complete.

Green ones,
are you serving gold and red
by providing contrast? Like
the artist's use of white,
deepening the experience for all?

A sacred contract
to remain backstage uttering
whispers of encouragement to
those playing leading roles this year?

Or, did you choose an
extended period of growth,
a slower response to your
natural calling? More time
to study your lines? Slower to
get out of your own way?

Oh, green ones,
the audience is gathering.
An excited hum fills the air.
We anxiously await your
moment on the stage.

Reverence

Over there,
in the foothills,
a small cluster of trees
cloaked in autumn colors:
red-leafed maples, yellow poplars,
Norway spruce, and ponderosa pine.

Standing there
in the midst of them all, two
dead Rocky Mountain White
Pines: brown and brittle from
life left long ago, towering over
the others, their skeletal limbs bare,
hanging limply close to the trunk,
pointing downward as if preparing
for an aerodynamic thrust skyward.

Two lifeless trees, ghost forms,
there amongst joyful life displayed
in brilliant autumn colors, as if
exaggerated for contrast to death.

The eyes fall upon the proud and
stately dead ones. Like hearing wisdom
passed down from the tribal elders,
they command one's full attention:
Spirit, recognized and respected.

They are protected and revered by
their tree community while roots rot
and loosen, freeing them to fall
groundward to decompose,
nourishing the earth as quietly
in death as they had in life.

Rocks from the Desert

Eyes turned to the
ground in concentrated
search for gifts from the
Earth: Indian shards,
arrowheads, rocks with
celestial color or rocks
washed smooth, left long
after the river flowed,
rocks that reflected a ray of
sun in recognition.

We walked for hours
under the strong Southwest
sun: heads down, pockets
full of sacred treasures taken
home to sit in a special place.

We found comfort in those
rocks. Rocks from the desert,
an austere, barren land, given
birth, surfaced and manifest
into solids of color, texture,
form and presence.

Chihuahuan Desert

Like the sky it reflects,
the Chihuahuan Desert
extends past what the
eye can see.

No valleys, no trees,
no protective canyon walls,
no sheltered spaces
to take refuge.
It is a flat land,
like a child's drawing,
without dimension to
reflect its depth.

Land with history
recorded upon it:
there for the bison,
the buffalo, the Anasazi,
giving way to the Spaniard
outfitted with horse and gun.

Followed by pioneers,
cattle, fences and
reservations for the Indian,
rounded up and driven,
like cattle, to places,
"out of the way".

The land is still
so much as it always was:
like an inherent reaction,
it recoiled from domestication
to protect its meager resources
from human exploitation.

A few, scattered houses
dot the landscape with
inhabitants as tough and
weathered as the land itself,
each seeking refuge from,
and requiring little,
of others.

And so it is,
the movement over
this land. They came in
waves over a waterless ocean:
few stayed, most
pushed father west
seeking the land of plenty.

Spirit

Returning

Home

Now, I Lead

Youngest of three:
sisters,
brunettes all!

Mother,
not sure I remember you:
taken by tuberculosis
before I could talk.

We sisters
somehow found our way
in a motherless world.

Followed my sisters,
I did: stealing boyfriends,
sharing a youthful trip to
Spain, becoming a teacher,
a mother.

Years pass.

Now, I lead,
a way-shower into
the infinite unknown.
While cancer
ravished my body,
grace thrived.

Spirit embolden,
I show my sisters the way,
lay rose petals in their path,
hold a lantern for them.
This, my sisters,
is my Gift to you.

Weeds and Roots

I grasped the weed securely
around its thin stem and
pulled straight up.
I could feel roots break away,
releasing into my hands.

My roots are breaking away,
leaving my life in my own hands.
Roots that extend deep
in several directions:
parents, home-place, hometown.
Pulled up.

Are roots like a tether,
holding one in place,
allowing no transcendence?
Or, do roots provide
stability, nourishment, direction?
All of it, I suppose.

Younger weeds pull up easily,
tender life, fluid, flexible.
Elder ones, thick of stem,
offer more resistance,
requiring leverage and
the metal edge of a hoe
to complete separation.
Life defined by time
not giving way easily.

Weed removed.
Vacant of life,
a hole remains.
Just as quickly,
backfill and cover,
nature's tilling,
preparation for new life.

Land may lie fallow,
as if in quiet reflection,
waiting for seed, sun, rain.
Or, life may spring forth
praising new opportunities to
create and express again.

Millie

Sky blue,
light, airy, infinite?
No.
Sky blue,
ribbed plastic tube
breathing artificial life.

Programmed,
twelve beats a moment,
"A safe number," the nurse says.
But she's doing twenty four,
still breaths she can call her own.

"Sorry we couldn't stop the seizures,"
she says.
Its her process, I think, let her be.
We will be with her,
however she needs to be.

Plastic tube, unhooked,
taken away.
We focus on the breath,
loud, labored, unsure.
An attempt to go it alone,
again.

A window to the sky,
slightly aside where the head lay,
Black birds fly by,
a message for Millie?
Reassurance.
The path through space time
is clear, White Light.

At the head,
a window opening to the sky,
at the feet, a door leading further
into a maze of walls and halls.
Will you walk or will you fly?

Space age technology
monitoring comatose body
in red, green and blue on black.
No instant replays this time,
a live account
recorded in a series
of beeps and colors.

Breath slowed,
colors changed.
Reddish white, feverish face,
mellowed into smooth, soft, buff.

One last short, intense seizure.
The exit.
Soul from body
propelled or drawn
from feet, through body and
out crown chakra,
leaving a trail of peace.

With White Light in sight,
the struggle stops.
In transition,
Millie lives in peace on Earth.
Face of an Angel,
mortal breath ceases.
Eternal, infinite-life continues.
Millie flies.

And the Grass Turned Green

December 7th,
cold skies gray.
Unexpected death, a shock.

Days later at Fort Logan,
the burial, honoring service to
her country, a First Lieutenant
many December 7th's ago.
We said our good-byes
before the casket was lowered
into newly prepared ground.

We went home,
emotions raw as
uncovered winter dirt.

We returned on a snowy
March day to say,
"Happy Birthday,"
not knowing Millie's
number in line, with only
a map and her spirit
to guide us, the new stone
eventually stood out from
amongst all the rest
in perfect formation.

The mud, pulled at the souls
of our feet, as if to say,
"Stay with me for a while."
Snow fell: cold winds blew.
We huddled together for
warmth and comfort,
torn between wanting to stay
and wanting to leave.

We went home,
cold, muddy and dazed,
spring nowhere in sight.

We returned Mother's Day,
warm sun, blue skies. We
walked directly to the stone.
Fragile, sprouting shoots of
green grass nestled closely
against the protective stone.

We went home
happy it was such a
beautiful day.

Returning unexpectedly
in June, another Mother
gone. A friend lies near,
but renewed opening to a
partially-healed wound.
Sun-blistered seedlings
lacking gentle, consistent
nurturing were
yellow and brown.

We returned in September,
summer fading into fall,
good news for Mom:
graduation in December.
Flickering green
fading blades huddled
closely around the stone.

We went home
knowing the first anniversary
was rapidly approaching and
only a few blades of grass
had taken hold.

December 7th,
one year later, celebrating
Millie at Pearl Harbor.

A nurse there once,
a soldier of mercy.
Lush green grass,
smell of the ocean,
flowers and a remembrance
cast into the waters of
times past and present.

Home again.
Graduation complete!

We returned,
for Holiday Greetings.
Evergreen wreath laid on
glistening white snow.

We went home,
quickly absorbed into
holiday bustle. No time
for quiet reflection.

We returned, March;
the second birthday.
Thick, yellow grass
replacing loose dirt,
soon to be lush green
as the sun rose
higher in the sky.
Millie's symbolic resting
place took hold.

We went home,
acknowledging
faith in nature.

Time passes,
seasons change,
wounds heal,
seeds germinate,
life continues,
we accept.

The transition is complete.

Doris A. Ervin
and
Barbara Duckworth

To Whom Much was Given

To whom much was given,
too much was expected.

She was bright, a genius;
let her figure it out.

Everything came so easily,
she didn't even have to try.
So efficient, effective.

We all depended on her.
She seemed so capable,
in charge.

Passed right by retirement,
still striving, more than ever.

In our binary world, there
is no off, only continual on.

We missed all kinds of signs:
an assortment of illnesses,
pain, exhaustion.

The doctors missed it,
time and time again.

Anxious to prescribe
rather than to diagnose:
pain pills were given so she
could get through her day,
masking the symptoms.

We all woke up
one day
after she collapsed
at work.

Stage 4 lymphoma.

She was always willing
to take it on. We were
always willing to let her.

Maybe it hadn't been
so easy for her, as
we were all so willing
to believe.

I Knew

I knew when I saw her
sleeping on the new sofa bed,
an unnatural, drug induced
sleep, pillows wedged around
her body to ease the yet
undiagnosed, cancerous pain.

I knew.

It was not a snuggled in,
comforting sleep.
It was a tense, stiff,
pretense of sleep;
horizontal waiting
for the unfolding of
an unknown illness.

I knew.

I knew that it had all gone
too far. The lead scout had
returned from behind enemy
lines, head down. There
was no possibility of retreat
from the front line, no truce,
no negotiating with an
unknown enemy.

I knew.

What do you do when
you know, and you know
that you know? Do you
call in reinforcements,
and rally the troops
around false hope? Do you
pretend to be positive in the
face of sure annihilation?
Do you kill the scout who
delivered the news?

      I knew

I knew a stealthy enemy was
marching forward, gaining
momentum with every
determined step.

      I knew.

The end was near.

He Killed Her

After forty years,
he fired two shots and
killed her.

Then,
drug her to the garage, and
threw her naked body out
by the trash.

Four days passed
in that house,
privacy unbroken,
a wife, naked of life,
an alcoholic husband.

He was, "One of the
kindest, gentlest people
we've ever known,"
they said.

She was,
"One of the brightest,
most intelligent people
we've ever known."

Some say it was money:
she a recent heiress.
Priorities forgotten?
Some say it was sex.
Loyalty forsaken?

A pattern set in motion
forty years ago, inextricably
weaving its way to conclusion.

Hands joined in mutual consent.
One covering for the other,
exchanging and shifting
enabling roles.

"I killed her. Now someone
needs to kill me,"
he said.

A pistol turned outward to
kill her demons, but unable to
turn it inward to kill his own.

Survival of self
the strongest of all emotions, or
righteousness over all?

Epilogue

I Am

I am unique –
like a rose opening
in the early morning
to its innate calling.

Unfolding,
to what only
it can be,
already is.

Yet,
just as I am
individual, I am
the same as every
other human being.

I can see it:
the knowingness
in their eyes; the
movement of their
bodies. I can hear it:
the comforting sound
of their voices.

All familiar.

Somewhere in the fog of
daylight, I stretch
into the day to become
both, unique, as me, and the
same as every 'other' being.

Reflections

As I sit here,
on the bank of
this slow moving river,
observing geese and ducks,
I know I want to
be like them:
beautiful, harmless
parts of the whole.

Floating serenely,
with an occasional
burst into flight
only to light again on the
constant, moving water.

www.ingramcontent.com/pod-product-compliance
Lightning Source LLC
Chambersburg PA
CBHW032214040426
42449CB00005B/590